DO ANIMALS THINK?

About consciousness in birds, dolphins, penguins, trees and other life forms

Vitali Milman

Copyright © 2021 Vitali Milman

All rights reserved.

Contents

Preface	vii
Birds	1
Australian magpie (1)	1
Kookaburra	4
Cockatoo	11
Australian magpie (2)	17
Our Tookie-Cookie	22
More stories about Birds, Suicidal Games, Revenge	25
Penguins	31
Magellanic Penguins	34
Dingo	38
Dolphins and Whales	41
"Thinking" trees	46
Microflora	50
Cells	53

Acknowledgments

I am infinitely grateful,

to Ludmila Milman for taking care of me and her advice,

to Michael Sonin for translating into English the articles of this book,

to Yonatan Milman, my grandson, for his excellent help in proofreading the Hebrew version of this book, and his advice about what material include in this book,

to Tatyana Petrova for her help with the files,

to Elena Vladimirskaya for her advice, support, and help in selecting the material, especially for the chapter "Cells",

to Tanya Preminger who help me to create this book,

and to all my friends who read these stories and expressed their opinion.

Preface

Let me start with one episode I observed a couple of months ago.

I was sitting in a parked car waiting for my wife Luda. In the middle of the street there was a median with grass and palm trees about every 10 meters. A smallish (but not small) bird flew onto this grass with a large piece of dry bread, a crust. It was an Israeli magpie.

It was sitting on the grass, breaking off pieces and eating them. Another similar bird flew up. It looked like they knew each other. The owner of the crust was clearly not going to share. The owner was letting the second bird watch it eat. It was also holding the crust to its side, not allowing the other bird to stand in front of the crust. After standing for a while, the second bird did not take any aggressive steps. It suddenly flew off and sat behind a palm tree about five meters away. It began to intensively dig something there but was doing it in a way that did not let the first bird see what it was digging, just its tail and the legs intensively tossing the soil.

The first bird was clearly intrigued — it stopped breaking off pieces of the crust and watched what the second bird was doing. Failing to figure it out, curiosity got the best of it — abandoning the crust, it flew over to join its mate behind the palm tree and have a look. As soon as it landed there, the digging bird took off, grabbed the abandoned crust, and flew away with it to another place (deceived!).

To sum it up, we have observed a conscious action of this second bird. It had a goal (to take possession of the crust) and an action plan to achieve this goal. The plan was successful, it worked.

All my long life I have been observing animals, and I wonder — what do they understand? Do they have consciousness? And what is consciousness? We, humans, understand only ourselves, and we usually observe the consciousness of animals through the behavior of domestic animals. But pets adapt to us. They understand us, not the other way around. We often know what they want, but that doesn't mean understanding.

In the Chapters "Birds", "Dingo", "Dolphins" of this book, I invite you to joint me in various episodes of my encounter with the animal kingdom, in which it was obvious to us that the animals demonstrated conscious behavior. They think! It will be like peeping through a crack into another room, another world, another civilization. Although more often, much more often, this other world will show us that it understands us and knows what we want to see.

However, I will not go beyond birds and mammals in these chapters. For me, it is complete darkness beyond that, total incomprehension. Although, surprisingly, even further out, I have come across trees that I understand a little, which, it looks, should "think".

I described them in the section, ""Thinking" Trees".

In my experience all these chapters are very suitable for children from age, say 10 and, definitely, till my age of 80 and, hopefully, beyond. The book contains two more chapters.

One is the chapter "Cells" where we discuss the behavior of cells of multicellular living being. Miracles were discovered recently in their life, and not to see consciousness in their behavior is just impossible! And another chapter about our microflora. These two additional chapters would be interesting starting older age, of, perhaps, 14. This is the estimate of my grandchildren.

Let me end this Preface just by my conclusion that consciousness accompanies any life, that any life must have consciousness, that life virtually equals consciousness. However, the question arises: what is consciousness? What do I mean when I say this word?

In fact, when we say the word "consciousness", we mean conscious actions. And we need to define what a conscious action is. What I mean by a conscious action is an action that entails a clear previously established goal that this action should achieve — a plan of action is conceived in advance, and the action follows this previously conceived plan.

Birds

I will start with another story about the same species of birds, but now it will be the

Australian magpie

In August 1988, we spent eight weeks in Canberra, Australia (that is, from mid-July to mid-September). Australia is an absolutely incredible world of birds, especially parrots. Judge for yourself;

This is not some bird park. This is a wild place, about 100 meters from the ocean and eight kilometers from an asphalt road. You take a country road to drive up here. Our car was the only one in this place. Some other car drove up later. You don't really see any birds when you arrive. But pulling out some bread is enough to sense movement in the trees. After standing for 5–10 minutes with your hand stretched out with bread, dozens and dozens of birds appear around you.

There are parrots of five or six different species. The ones sitting on Luda are of the same species, and this is no coincidence. This happened every time we went there. The species of parrots that first worked up the courage to flock from the trees and fly up to the bread/Luda will occupy this premium space. The rest will be picking up the crumbs on the ground. By the way, even more than bread, these parrots love grapes. You get a sense that they get drunk from them. Of course, the fact that they are not afraid of this huge "monster" — a human — and know that it poses no danger, indicates a certain level of intelligence.

But now I am talking about a very intelligent bird, and once again we have come to the magpie, this time the Australian magpie. We were renting a small house on the outskirts of Canberra. There were always birds in the small area in front of the entrance. Although there were fewer parrots in this place. There were a lot of them on the university campus. Of course, our children, nine-year-old Anat and 11-year-old Emanuel, fed the birds a little. There was even some kind of a small feeder on the ground a couple of meters from the entrance.

We had already been living there for a while, and the birds were also used to us, although they scattered when we walked past them. Once, fairly early in the morning, there was a small knock on the door. We were all downstairs already, not far from the entrance. Luda went to open the door.

Our front door opened into an entrance hall, about two by two meters, which led into the living room through an open entryway. Luda opened the door and saw no one. She then looked down and saw a bird standing by the entrance! It was the bird who knocked on the door! We were all nearby but standing in the living room. Luda moved away. And the bird slowly, in no haste, came in and made a circle around the entrance hall.

It was obvious that the bird was terribly nervous. It even relieved itself a little on the floor along the way, out of fear. But it made this journey and went back to the porch. None of us moved. The bird breathed a sigh of relief (this was my interpretation, but it was an obvious one). It then glanced at us again and jumped off the porch. The feat was over. It went to the feeder. And we realized that it showed all the birds that were watching from all sides that this was its place now. The bird claimed it and was now the master. And from that point on, all the other birds waited for it to finish its meal and move away from the feeder. And then the other birds could eat too.

Once again, we see a clearly set goal, a complex and risky plan, and its rigorous implementation. What can we learn from this story about this civilization, the civilization of Australian magpies? I will later return to the Australian magpies of a slightly different type. They will surprise us again. But for now, I will move on to another Australian bird,

Kookaburra

This is a completely unusual bird, perhaps the most intellectual and intelligent bird in existence.

I will start with a description of our acquaintance.

As I mentioned above, in 1988, we spent some time in Australia. One day we went to a Canberra city park for a picnic. We were sitting at a table with the children. The food was on the table. I noticed some bird on a tree branch next to the table. It was completely unattractive in appearance. No bright colors. And there was absolutely no inkling that it was trying to grab any food from us (we once had an incident of this sort when a bird watching us suddenly swooped down and grabbed a huge piece of cheese from us). The pose of this bird conveyed curiosity. It was enjoying watching the family picnic. Very strange that it did occur to me then. Perhaps this was because its eyes were large, human-like, not the dots that many birds have. But I had not yet noticed that at the time. After watching for a little while, and having noticed my interest in it, the bird flew away.

Somehow, it remained in my memory. After a long time, more than a year later, already back in Israel, there was an ornithology professor (bird expert) at one of the parties. And I immediately remembered this strange, seemingly unremarkable bird. I asked him. Mind you, I was feeling very awkward because there was nothing I could tell about the bird. Well, it was some kind of bird that I could not describe and whose name I did not know. So I just said that a certain bird caught my interest. That was enough for him. He immediately said that it was kookaburra, an extremely intelligent bird about which we still know very little. It leads a social life, it even knows its nephews and visits them. That is, it was simply the bird's intellectual disposition that caught my attention.

The Aboriginal people just love it when this bird settles near their village. In the morning it screams something like koo-ka-ba-ra, which is where its name comes from. The Aboriginal people call it kookaburra laughter. We have never heard a single sound coming from it. Kookaburra eats meat. It eradicates snakes in the area where it lives. It eats them. The hunting method is as follows. It grabs the snake near the head (as people try to do), then soars into the air and throws the snake onto rocks. If this does not kill the snake the first time around, the kookaburra repeats. Its reaction speed is surreal. We saw it once. And it outmaneuvers the snake.

After 1988, we made short visits to Australia a couple more times, but we never encountered kookaburras. In 2002, we came to Canberra again for two months. All this time, our balcony was full of different birds, mostly cockatoos. I will write about this later. But the kookaburra did not appear until 10–12 days before our departure. One early morning, say at 7 a.m., Luda came out of the bedroom into the living room, walked up to the balcony, and called me: "Vitaly, there is a new bird on the tree across from us". Naturally, I immediately jumped up to have a look and saw the kookaburra. I started rushing about and grabbed the camera, afraid to miss it, afraid that it would fly away. Very slowly I opened the balcony door and began to take pictures while standing in the doorway. Kookaburra was sitting and looking at me. Then it took off and landed right on the balcony railing, facing me. The gesture was obviously an invitation to take pictures. I took a few more pictures. It would turn in different directions. Then, looking at me, it started to open and close its mouth! This was another obvious universal sign — it was now time to feed it. We happened to have slices of raw meat, the best food for kookaburra. Luda quickly brought a bowl of this meat. Luda took a slice of meat and was about to put it on the railing. Kookaburra reached out to take the meat straight from Luda's hands. But Luda got scared and pulled her hand away. That was it — never again did the kookaburra try to take meat from her hands.

It patiently waited for Luda to put the meat on the railing.

Later Luda gave the kookaburra the bowl with meat, and it ate straight from the bowl.

Such was this idyllic scene, right from the first minute of acquaintance! For a month and a half we fed the cockatoos (I will tell you later what that came to), but they were still afraid to let us closer than about a meter.

The complete lack of fear in kookaburra was simply evidence of its understanding that there was no danger.

Finally, the kookaburra was full. How do you think the bird showed this and expressed its gratitude?

Have a look:

It turned its back to us to demonstrate its friendship, to show that it was not afraid of us. We were inches away. By the way, during all this time, all the other birds — the cockatoos and others — looked on from the trees, they did not dare to approach the kookaburra. An exception took place the next day. And this is a new remarkable story. The next day, the kookaburra showed up at exactly the same time as on the first occasion. It immediately sat down on the railing, and the feeding process began. However, two things happened.

The first event was a clash that took place between the kookaburra and the Australian magpie who had been feeding on our balcony for a month and considered the balcony its turf. And suddenly its food was being taken away! It turned out that the magpie also liked to eat meat, something I was not aware of before this incident. And we used to feed it with bread, which the cockatoos also ate. Although the cockatoos liked seeds.

I will talk about this separately, later, in the story about this wonderful bird, also of great intelligence. But still not quite the kookaburra. The kookaburra just brushed it off. Now for the second event. Our kookaburra finished its meal and flew away. But twenty minutes later another kookaburra flew over, a little one. I think our adult kookaburra gave our address to its nephew.

For some reason, I do not think this was its child. The next day we took pleasure in the company of the kookaburra. Notice the delicate dialogue between Luda and the kookaburra.

After that, we flew off for a week to the tropical zone for a brief scientific visit. A week later, we returned for two days and then flew out of Australia. During the week we were away, we were worried whether the kookaburra would return, whether it would wait for a week. It waited. In the morning, at the same time, it flew up to check if we had returned.

This is already the farewell breakfast. We flew away that morning. I wonder how long it kept flying by to see if we were back. Note its eyes. You can compare later when I show you the cockatoo. The cockatoo's eyes are dots, whereas the kookaburra's eyes have human-like structure.

I am moving on to the story about the

Cockatoo

In the photo on the left, the cockatoo is agitated and tense. You can see this by its raised crest. In the photo on the right, it is eating calmly.

Here is a strange thing. On Wikipedia, I read that these cockatoos live about 40 years. However, back in 1988, we visited the cockatoo circus with our young children Anat and Emanuel. There we were told that they live over 100 years, and that they keep getting smarter all the time. In confirmation, they demonstrated the capabilities of cockatoos of different ages. At first there were the 30-year-olds, then the 40- to 50-year-olds; after them, cockatoos about 60, 70, and finally 80 years of age. And indeed, the level increased to an absolutely incredible degree of complexity and, in fact, also performance. For some reason, I have more faith in the people who interacted with them.

Cockatoos live and move around in flocks. I have seen flocks of, I think, up to a hundred birds. When they fly, they make terribly loud screams. Moreover, those screams are very ugly, a kind of guttural croaking. They are individualists and egoists (according to our observations)

They took a while to appear on our balcony. Their standard food is seeds or bread. We would leave some on the balcony, and gradually they began to wait for the treats. They usually flew over in large numbers, but a couple of them became our regular guests. In order for them not to quarrel, we poured several heaps of seeds, but there were times when one of them tried to take over more than one heap. Battles of intrigue were played out in front of us. But overall, they got along relatively well.

They sometimes ate as in the photo on the left, but more often as in the one on the right, that is, looking in opposite directions so as not to fight. Once, after they were already in the habit of eating regularly on our balcony for some time, there was a knock on the window early in the morning.

I have to explain the layout of the rooms. We had a living room with a balcony where all the events with the birds took place. From this living room there was a door to another room with one window adjacent to the balcony. However, this window had shutters that were always closed. The birds could never see us in this room! But somehow they knew that we slept there. And they knocked on our window: "It's morning already, where is our breakfast?" Luda got up and went to give them seeds so that they would let us get some more sleep. That's how smart these birds were. They figured out where to find us and knocked on the window if we were late.

I once observed a strange story in the life of cockatoos, which I have not been able to decipher. An adult cockatoo was sitting on the edge of our railing, pressed against the wall. A smaller cockatoo, probably her baby, snuggled up to her. The young of these birds grow quickly and they are close to adult birds in size. He was obviously whimpering. He was muttering, asking his mom for something. (By the way, I am assigning the gender completely arbitrarily here — this one is male and that one is female. I do not know and cannot distinguish gender in birds.)

The adult cockatoo, the mom, occasionally responded. This was an absolutely typical scene of a mom and a whimpering baby, just like humans. It went on for a long time, and I do not know how it ended, because I left the balcony, and when I returned, they were not there. I was very curious what the child could have been asking from his mother. There was plenty of food around on the balcony. So, the cockatoo "shall not live by bread alone".

Sometime toward the end of our stay in Canberra, we learned that we could buy special treats for cockatoos in stores. Something they love. It is a certain concentrated mix of different types of nuts, possibly slightly sweetened, attached to a plastic stick. Naturally, we bought some

In the photo you can see this stick, but almost all the food from it has already been eaten. This stick has a hook to tie it to a tree. We meant for the cockatoos to sit on the branches and feast on it. However, the very first cockatoo that flew up, after tinkering for a minute, managed to remove it from the tree and appropriated it.

DO ANIMALS THINK?

We tied it a second time and tried very hard to make it difficult (in my view, impossible) to remove, but I was mistaken. In the top right photo, you can see the cockatoo trying to get to the bar, and the photo on the left shows the cockatoo ruminating about the task.

I don't know how, but after a while this entire edible bar was in its hands (that is, its feet). And then on the third attempt, I decided to tie it to the back of a chair.

You can see this in the photo below. And you see the cockatoo taking the most suitable spot. I will explain.

It could not sit on top of the back of the chair, as the chair would tip over (one of the cockatoos tried it). Sitting on the other side was "dangerous", as its back would be facing us.

Sitting on the seat of the chair was also dangerous since it couldn't take off quickly. So the only spot is occupied by this cockatoo. In the adjacent photo, you can see the cockatoo trying to reach for the sweets. A large group of other cockatoos is watching the attempts of the first cockatoo.

And now the denouement. The first cockatoo managed to break off pieces of the delicacy with its foot. However, it did not immediately put the second piece in its mouth and kept it in its foot. At that point, the cockatoo sitting next to it snatched this piece from its foot and quickly stuffed it into its own mouth. I have it filmed on video.

DO ANIMALS THINK?

After this drama, that very first cockatoo could no longer stand it. It sat down on the seat of the chair, and after a bit of work, managed to tear off the entire bar from the chair and flew away with it. We didn't want to come closer and never learned how the bird tore it off. Perhaps their beak could bite through the rope we used to tie this bar.

In the story about kookaburra, I promised to come back to another bird, the

Australian magpie (2),

which I already wrote about. This magpie here is a little different from the one I wrote about from our visit to Canberra in 1988.

Note the white patch on the head of both magpies. The one I'm talking about now has the slightly larger white patch.

These birds sing well and were spectacular at catching on the fly pieces of bread that Luda loved to throw for them. Only very recently I learned that in 2017 this bird won the Bird of the Year 2017 online competition. And here is what was written about its victory: "It resembles a magpie in appearance and is known for its many-voiced morning singing. But more recognizable than its voice are this bird's swift swooping attacks on suspiciously approaching subjects, especially during the incubation period".

We have certainly observed both of these traits. Because of them, my wife nicknamed one of the two birds of this type that visited us regularly, a songstress, and also a sniper. In the mornings, when it sang invitingly, waiting for food (at the time when the cockatoos knocked on the window), Luda would say: "the songstress has come". But when she threw bread for the bird, the same songstress would become a sniper.

Actually, it was one of the two such birds that had these talents — I don't know if it was a female or a male.

We already understand that wishing to claim its spot on this balcony and with us, this magpie also thought about entering our room. But it didn't have the courage. It stood for a while at the entrance from the balcony into the room. But it only worked up the courage to eat while standing on the doorstep. On the other hand, it offered its own friendship test. It turned around and stood with its back to us, as the kookaburra did. But in this case, we were at a much farther distance from the bird. I included its photo, with its back to us, above.

And now the story of the fight between the kookaburra and our songstress, which I mentioned in the story about the kookaburra. We have a video of this. I will now provide a few shots from this video. On the first two photos, the magpie is slowly moving closer to the kookaburra, who keeps its back to the magpie and doesn't even wish to acknowledge its presence. But when the magpie came too close, there was a sudden, very quick move by the kookaburra, and the magpie retreated, angry but fearful

The magpie then steadied itself and sang its very beautiful "battle song". The kookaburra looked on only with curiosity and without any tension.

The magpie is preparing another attempt to approach the food, but once again, the kookaburra just makes a quick move, and the magpie flies away to another side of the balcony.

What the next photo below depicts is already the finale. The magpie realizes that it has lost and is just waiting for the kookaburra's departure.

As I already described in the story about the kookaburra, on the first day when it flew over, it ate peacefully and flew away. All the birds that usually spent the morning on our balcony watched this from a tree. I wasn't really expecting a conflict, because we fed them bread and seeds, and the kookaburra meat.

However, I did not know that the magpie also likes meat, and even much more than the bread which we fed it. On the second day of kookaburra's visits, the magpie could no longer stand it. It apparently believed that the kookaburra was just flying by and would not take its place on this balcony in the future. And there it was for the second day in a row. The kookaburra was turning into a permanent member of this community and taking meat away from the magpie.

So, while the kookaburra was eating meat and all the birds were respectfully sitting on the tree and watching, our magpie flew up and sat on the balcony railing, but about a meter or one and a half from the kookaburra. And it sang its battle song, a very beautiful one. I think I recorded it. But that video only shows the second short song between the two attack attempts. After that the magpie began to approach the kookaburra. Zero attention from kookaburra as it continues to eat calmly.

When the magpie approached to the distance of a peck, the kookaburra made a lightning movement with its head in the magpie's direction, and the magpie flew away in fright. Incidentally, all of this was recorded on video in full. The magpie sat on the other side of the balcony and watched the calm dining of the kookaburra. This is reflected in the photo above. I think she sang another song. When the kookaburra flew away, we tried to calm and feed the songstress.

I should note that a kookaburra is smaller than a magpie and much smaller than a cockatoo. But the mind determines the status for birds too

Our Tookie-Cookie

About 20 years ago, a parrot lived with us for a whole year. It was a gift from one of Anat's friends. However, Anat did not find much time to communicate with him. And Luda took it upon herself to care for him. His appreciation and love are reflected in the photo on the left, and his favorite position is in the one on the right.

As a result, the only family member to whom the parrot did not like to come was Anat. He loved Emanuel and played certain games with me.

He quickly realized that I did not like him sitting on frames of paintings. To that end, he would sit on some frame at the far end of the room. He looked at me and waited. I could not get to him. Our ritual was as follows. I would take a long stick and walk toward him. As I approached, he would fly to another painting across the room. This would continue several times, but not too many. He correctly understood that enough was enough and found himself something else to do. For example, he might sit on a frame without a painting in it, specially prepared for him. We got this parrot when he was about a month old. His scientific name is cockatiel and he is also known as weiro bird or quarrion. This is a branch of the cockatoo family that originates from Australia.

In a very short time, Luda taught him to speak perfectly. By the way, it was a male. The female's behavior is completely different, and they usually don't speak. Back to the main theme of my entire story, the consciousness of this bird, our Tookie-Cookie understood what he was saying. For example, "Good morning" (in Hebrew, "boker tov"; in reality, "boker, boker, boker tov") was only spoken in the morning. When I phoned from the United States, after a while I could hear someone next to Luda saying: "enough, Luda, enough" (in Hebrew, "maspik, Luda, maspik"). That was our Tookie-Cookie reckoning that he was not being paid due attention. Luda taught him to sing.

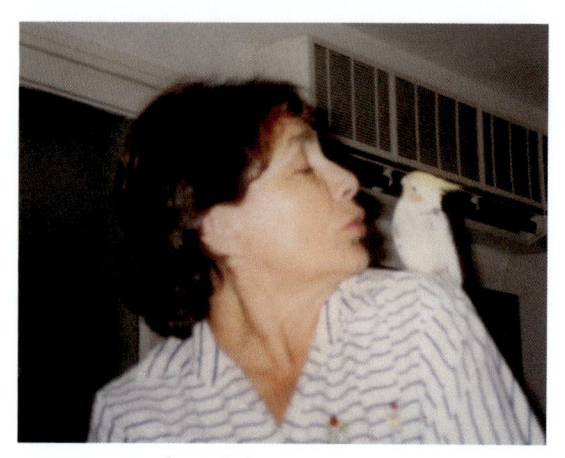

Luda Giving a Lesson

This was perhaps the most startling part. He whistled The Magic Flute by Mozart spectacularly. Our friends and acquaintances would come to listen. For some reason I thought that the famous song from the movie "The Bridge on the River Kwai", whistled in the movie by the colonel, would be very easy for him to memorize and perform. But it turned out to be difficult. However, the parrot tried very hard — he rehearsed it many times on his own. Somewhere in the middle of the musical piece, he would break into Mozart. But he would often start over. Eventually, he was able to whistle it, but it was an effort. That's the kind of genius Tookie-Cookie was. Unfortunately, one night at 11 p.m., Luda went out onto the back balcony with him on her shoulder, stumbled, and he flew out into the darkness. He kept flying over us for a long time, but then flew somewhere else. This was during our Israeli winter, but that night happened to be cold, below +10 degrees Celsius. We don't know what happened to him. Our huge mistake was that we never showed him our house from the outside. And even if he survived that first night, he could not figure out where to return.

We were told that if we brought our parrot company, he would stop talking to us. They would be busy with each other. This is why I would not know what his behavior is like in the company of parrots like him. However, we put up a mirror for him. At first, it was in his cage. The parrot would peer in from the other side to see the companion, but quickly realized that it was he himself in the mirror. But still, he often approached it and talked to himself, as in the photo:

More stories about Birds, Suicidal games, Revenge.

Another story about birds that I want to mention happened in India. We were staying overnight on the university campus, and when it was already dark outside, we decided to go for a walk outside the campus gates. We were walking along the alley toward the exit and could not talk. The trees along the alley were full of birds that made incredible noise. Their chirping was so intense that it was impossible to talk. We walked for about five minutes outside the gate and then walked back. We were walking along the alley and the silence buzzed in our ears. Absolute silence. The birds went to sleep. They had been making incredible noise, but suddenly, as if by order, they fell silent at once.

Suddenly, I recall another amazing story involving birds. It happened in the mid-sixties. Once again, I was at a conference in Central Asia, in Uzbekistan, in one of the big cities. This place was surrounded by a mountainous terrain, and a mathematician acquaintance of mine took a group of two or three of us for a drive in his car around the countryside outside the city. We were driving along a straight road through hills and mountains. The road had been cut through them, so every 100 or 150 meters there were vertical earthy cliffs on both sides of the car, the remains of a cut hill. We were driving at a speed of about 100 kilometers per hour. And every time we drove through these passages, a flock of birds would fly over from the cliff on one side to the opposite one, right in front of our car. Just as we were passing through, right in front of the windshield of the car. It was obviously a game, perhaps even a competition between the birds to see who would fly off later and closer to the car. This is how kids played in my childhood on the roads in the villages. A deadly game. My wife recounted to me how she participated in these games. And one bird didn't make it, and we struck it down. It was a real pity. But it was too late to slow down — the birds would fly off right in front of the car when we were already in this narrow passage. Playing with death (or a competition to the death?).

Does this signify consciousness? I think YES, and a high-level one. By the way, these were small birds, similar to sparrows.

And the last story in this section.

My friend, professor of medicine Elena (Lena) Vladimirskaya, told me an interesting story about the common raven, another extremely intelligent bird.

This is a story of revenge. Perhaps (I'm even sure of this) revenge is a sure sign of consciousness. Lena had a female friend who lived in the same building and had a very beautiful cat. One morning, this cat was found dead near the building entrance. It was pecked to death by birds — ravens — who were still flying around. The cat could not escape in time. One of the neighbors recounted that two days earlier he had seen this cat in a tree ravaging a raven's nest. I have also heard of other similar cases.

While on the subject of revenge as a derivative of consciousness, I would also like to discuss another human-like manifestation of consciousness, humor, and how it relates to consciousness, its role in consciousness. Pause to think if you can answer the question of what humor is. Is it a derivative of consciousness? I must honestly say that I thought about this question for a very long time. And my realization was unexpected. I suddenly realized that humor is akin to mimicry. Mimicry is a well-known phenomenon. It is animals' adaptation against their enemies. It is manifested in different ways. Some, such as chameleons, change their color and become almost invisible to their enemies. Others make sounds that their enemies fear. Animals adapt to defend themselves against enemies by pretending to be someone/something else if they cannot defeat them. Is this a manifestation of consciousness? I do not know. Zoologists prefer to think of this as a "reflex", something lower than consciousness, but I would classify it as consciousness.

And now on to humor. Humor is a defensive reaction against "friends", in contrast to mimicry, which serves this function against "enemies". I think hearing this for the first time is puzzling. So let's start with an example. Think of a group of friends where a conflict suddenly emerges, and a fight is about to break out. They are about to fight, when one of them tells a funny story, and everyone laughs. And they have already forgotten about the impending fight.

I think a lot of people have been in such situations early in life. So humor restores calmness in spontaneous conflicts. This is a very important quality, undoubtedly related to consciousness. Conflicts are related to consciousness, and humor that extinguishes them all the more so.

I tried to see what I would consider humor in the animal world. It is difficult. Apparently, you need to be too deep inside that world. Recently, I came across two different stories in which the humor of the animals was evident, at least in our human understanding. One of them describes a raven's revenge, which was carried out with incredible humor. The incident was observed and described by the writer Julia Wiener. However, this text is unfortunately only available in Russian, and I will try to retell the story in my own words. (The original story can be read at:

https://www.facebook.com/julia.wiener.94/posts/3817388628290373.

A boy of about twelve was walking along the path in the park and tossed a stale pita flatbread lying on the path at a raven. The flatbread grazed the raven's tail. (As we will see, this angered the raven.) The boy leisurely walked on, while the raven grabbed this pita from the ground. But it did not fly away with the flatbread to eat it — the raven immersed the pita into a puddle next to the path, stood on it with its two feet so that it got thoroughly soaked, grabbed it with its beak, and flew after the boy. After making a small circle over the boy, apparently taking aim, the raven opened its beak, and the pita fell right on the boy's head — the soaked and crumbling flatbread. It was a spectacular act of revenge. By human standards, it even showed a sense of humor. At least the passersby, according to Wiener's story, laughed, while the boy was very upset. Later, the raven calmly picked up the pieces of pita, so it didn't lose its food either.

Another story is captured in the video where a monkey taunts two tiger cubs. This video can be viewed at:
https://www.youtube.com/watch?v=NRyGzlf6SpQ

The video may have been shot in some park or nature reserve. The monkey, possibly an infant, was amusing itself by taunting two tiger cubs. It would grab them by the ear or by the tail, and then quickly climb up the tree. At times, the monkey pretended to be sitting peacefully on the ground, and when the cubs sneaked up, it managed to grab one of the cubs by the ear before quickly scaling the tree. The monkey was clearly teasing and taunting them a little.

Let me show you a few shots from that video. On the first photo the intentions seem peaceful. But then you see . . .

And again, just an observer, but then:

And again:

Still Birds but Penguins

In 2006, we visited Melbourne and an oceanfront penguin sanctuary near Melbourne.

By the way, despite a very hot day, being on the ocean shore after dark feels very cold, and to see the penguins you need to be there in the dark. We were warned of this and had blankets. The place from which we took pictures has wooden benches, and many spectators wait for darkness. The birds that we see in the photo disappear, and as soon as it gets dark, penguins begin to emerge from the foam of the waves. It is a very entertaining sight. They hide in the incoming wave, and then quickly run into the bushes, which begin exactly where the photo ends. Their height is approximately 33 cm (but their body length is 43 cm). This is the smallest species of penguin. So, wave after wave throws groups of penguins ashore. This continues late into the night. Having run into the bushes, the penguins begin to climb up the trail. The trail quickly becomes a track along which they walk to their burrow homes. In the photo we see them walking in groups along this track.

Extending from the shore inland along the penguin track, there is a wooden suspension path built for us, the spectators. So, having watched enough of their exodus from the ocean, we walk along this wooden path and observe the penguins walking. The penguin town is everywhere around us. Branching from the main track are smaller tracks that turn into tiny ones. Penguin burrows are everywhere along these tracks and trails. And there are small heads of children popping out everywhere, waiting for their family with food.

You know, of course, that penguins carry food in their belly. They open their mouths, their young put their mouths in mom's (or dad's) mouth, and mom regurgitates the fish. So the penguins are carrying a load and it is difficult for them to walk. This is why, after walking some distance, they stop and rest. It is incredibly amusing how they stop all of a sudden and all together. They freeze, each in its own position, as if by order. Not a movement for some time, as if caught by an "order" that came from some place unknown.

And then suddenly they start moving, all together. When one of them reaches its trail, it turns onto it, and there is a sense that the penguin is taking its leave of the rest, who continue to walk along the main track. Of course, as in any society, there is no equality. Some live close to the ocean and in good thickets, while others have to walk to a place very far away that is also a bad one.

I want to describe one scene, possibly a tragic one. Right next to us, but down on the penguin track (we were standing on the wooden suspension bridge above), there were two baby penguins. They nearly matched an adult penguin in size, but their "fur" was different. Their burrow was nearby, and they teetered between standing near it and running out onto the track. They were constantly squeaking — I think they were crying. They were obviously very hungry. And they ran to every passing group of penguins asking for food. They were coming onto them with their mouths open. But the adult penguins would steer away, walk around them, and continue along to their children. Only once did one mother take pity on them and let each take something from her mouth. This was not at all enough for the little ones, and they continued to beg for food from the following groups. We approached a nearby attendant and drew her attention to this pair. She told us that their family might still come, and that some stay in the ocean for more than a day if their hunt was unsuccessful. But she made a note of them to help after a while. She told us that they keep an eye on these things. For some reason, I did not feel assured, but we left hopeful.

And now a question. Was the one penguin sharing food with others' babies a conscious act?

We will now leap to the penguins of Argentina, the so-called

Magellanic Penguins

In the winter 2010, we traveled on the Celebrity Infinity cruise ship around South America. Two weeks, a fantastic trip. We started in Santiago, rounded South America through the Strait of Magellan, stopped in some nearly deserted place in Argentina, and traveled an hour by bus to the penguin town. The road was a good one, a highway, so this was probably 100 kilometers south of the port. The place is one of the national parks of Argentina. Park staff estimate that this place, a real town, is home to about two million penguins. From what we have seen, this appears to be a correct estimate.

As in Melbourne, we first walked for a long time along a wooden path, built slightly above the ground so as not to interfere with the penguins passing under it. Although at some point it ended, and we could walk on the ground. There were penguins walking everywhere among us — they would walk to the ocean for food and return with food to their burrows, where the children were waiting for them. There were burrows all around, and there were baby penguins standing near them

Here are the penguins walking to and from the ocean.

And here you see "social inequality". The family on the left lives in ideal conditions: the burrow is shielded with trees from the attacks of birds of prey from above, and incidentally it is very close to the ocean, where they have to go for food.

The photo on the right shows a completely marginal family: their burrow is open to any predator, and the children must hide in the burrow very quickly in case of danger. They are easy prey. And the location is far from the ocean

In the photo on the left there is a family again. Their place is quite good, but not the best. There are bushes around, and the ocean is not far away.

Note that the cubs are always behind their mother. The adult penguin has a reddish patch over its nose, which the cubs do not have. The photo on the right shows a general view of their town, stretching very far into the distance. By the way, we have seen families with three cubs

This is their seashore where they come to the water for food and leave the water to go "home". They also spend a long time standing on the shore, and you get a feeling that they are communicating with each other in some way. The photo below is larger and offers a better view of some details of their behavior.

As I bid farewell to the birds in my narrative, I want to show their legendary huddles:

DO ANIMALS THINK?

And a closer-up view of another huddle (these are not penguins):

This is on the islands roughly opposite the penguin town.

Dingo

We crossed paths with the dingo in the center of Australia, at Ayers Rock (called Uluru by the Aboriginal people).

What you see in the picture is 348 meters high, 3.6 kilometers long, and 2.4 kilometers at its widest point. And for tens of kilometers around is flat Earth! This is a wild place, sacred to the Aboriginal people. 15 kilometers away there is a purpose-built cultural center that offers the opportunity to stay overnight to visit this Monolith. Another 450 kilometers away is the small town of Alice Springs, where you can travel by plane. It is exactly 2,000 kilometers south of the city of Darwin, which is on the coast of Australia. 25 kilometers toward Darwin, the Southern Tropic (Tropic of Capricorn) passes along the highway. My family and I drove up to have our picture taken on this line.

To get a feel for this place, I will mention that at the point where this highway leaves Alice Springs heading toward Darwin, there is a huge sign: 1,000 kilometers to the next gas station (halfway to Darwin). Such was this place back in 1988.

Back to the dingo. We were driven to Ayers Rock with a minibus tour. And then they "forgot" to pick us up! Just like that, and we were there with two children who were still very young at the time. I don't wish to call up this memory and write about it, but I understood what kind of people England populated

Australia with. We couldn't believe it, and just waited another hour or two, without water or anything. Everything was on the bus. The last tours ended by noon, and there were only a couple of such late tours remaining.

Eventually, we approached a police officer, who was also due to leave. Amazed and incensed, he used a radiotelephone to find this vile driver. This is how we got picked up from that place. But before we did, we encountered a dingo.

We were lucky that we stayed behind and there were only another five or six people around. We were standing near the Rock, and this small group of people was about 10 meters away. And there was a little yellow dog with these people, running between them. A very cute little dog. Just a little pet dog that came with these people. I was watching it in delight, while the dog was glancing at me. And suddenly I realized that it was a dingo! I have read that they pretend to be pet dogs, looking for something to snatch.

There are cases known of babies being grabbed and carried away into the desert. There is even a movie about it. So I figured it out. Perhaps my gaze had changed, because the dingo immediately realized that it had been discovered. Its gaze changed — instantly it turned into a wild beast, one that I would have been afraid to run into. It rushed to the Rock to run around us along the top and ran off into the flat desert plain covered with yellowish sunburnt grass. Just a few meters from the Rock you could no longer make it out. It seems to me that this group of people that the dingo was running between never realized what happened.

An amazing level of pretense performed with artistry, and then a brutal beast escaping possible pursuit. Undoubtedly conscious behavior! Conscious mimicry. Although this, of course, is not quite mimicry.

Dolphins and a Little about Whales

I'll start with whales because this will be brief. I have only had one observation of conscious behavior of whales, and I have also observed a whale circus where one could argue "consciousness" versus "training". Although perhaps good training simply involves understanding the consciousness of the animal and how to communicate with it.

I think it was the summer of 2002. The Pacific Institute for the Mathematical Sciences in Vancouver (PIMS) had a special summer semester where I was one of the directors. Sometime in August, we took a short vacation and went to a small place on the ocean shore. This was a place from where many small tourist boats went out to the ocean every day to watch whales. You could observe various types of whales at this location. And we were lucky indeed — we saw two types of whales. Since there are a lot of boats, they go to different places and tell each other on the radio if they suddenly see whales. This greatly increases the likelihood of success. In the beginning we saw whales producing spouts. We sailed very close to them. They feed on plankton and are very large in size. Their spouts are magnificent, and we thoroughly enjoyed them. And then a radio message came in that there were killer whales somewhere not far away.

It is difficult to catch sight of them, as they move quickly over great distances. This was lucky, and we immediately sailed there at full speed. When we arrived at the site, we did indeed see a couple of whales in the distance, which broke the surface and then dived back in. That was it, we didn't see anything else. We were all huddling on the deck, looking in all directions. And there was nothing.

A long time passed, maybe 10 or 15 minutes, perhaps even longer. We felt that our luck ran out just about before it started. And suddenly (!!) just meters from our boat, I think less than five meters, two huge whales simultaneously broke the surface and soared into the air. As in the photo, but only in parallel, together, perfectly coordinated, in the same (identical) position. They were the size of our boat; it seemed to me that they were bigger than 10 meters. Although I have read that this is their maximum size.

Having this whopper next to us was even scary. After splashing water on us, they dived slightly against the line of our motion. I was even afraid of a collision, but they were moving much faster than us. Their tails were going calmly into the water, and I even managed to take a photo of them. Unfortunately, the time of digital photography was yet to come, and I do not know how to find these images now. So I borrowed them from the internet (thanks).

We kept waiting for a long time, looking around. But having demonstrated themselves, they swam so far that it was impossible to see where they surfaced next. It is quite obvious that this simultaneous "flight" in the air was performed for our benefit. It was a conscious demonstration. We thank them for that.

Two years ago, we visited the Canary Islands. Our cruise stopped at the island of Tenerife and we visited Loro Park to see a whale show on that island. The whales tried very hard and everything was fine. Toward the end of the show, the trainer gave the whale the freedom to have some fun. I don't remember what he called it. At the entrance we were given light plastic raincoats. The whale began to swim in a circle of a huge aquarium and used its tail to douse us with water. I thought I was sitting far enough away that the water would not reach me. But it doused us from head to toe. What I noted for myself was that the whale clearly enjoyed this exercise. It performed the other tricks because it had to. But now the whale was working with all its heart, with full enthusiasm. And when the whale was given a signal to stop, it made one more round and doused us with water again. I wonder if this was revenge for being forced to work, or humor?

I am moving on to the dolphin stories.

I first encountered dolphins in person around 1964–1965. I was at the first organized mathematical school in Katsiveli, Crimea. This place had the Institute of Oceanology of the Soviet Academy of Sciences. Its director was an expert, very famous in Russia, in seas and oceans, primarily dealing with weather conditions, squalls, and storms. To study waves, there was a large pool in the form of a thick ring at the site. The walls were glass, and one could be inside and observe, for example, the waves that were specially created from the inside. This was the time when rumors began to circulate that the Americans were training dolphins for use in military operations. Russia was not to be left behind.

So, it was decided to conduct experiments on dolphins in this ring pool. We, the mathematicians of this school, transported dolphins in trucks from the sea to this pool. Several friends and I were transporting the first three dolphins. It turned out that the truck had nails sticking out and one dolphin was injured. We poured water on them from above while driving. They are very sensitive to the sun. They were unwell. But they tried harder than us not to injure us accidentally with their sharp teeth. There was no resistance, only help from the dolphins. And their gaze was understanding and kind. Once we dropped the first three into the pool, and they started swimming in a circle, the wounded dolphin could not swim alone, so the other two supported it from the sides. The three of them were swimming together. Once the other dolphins were brought in, they would switch and lead this injured dolphin, always in pairs, from two sides. Such was their intelligence, their mutual support. The story ended tragically. All dolphins, one by one, eventually perished. Everything was unfit for the experiment.

Our second very close encounter with dolphins was a happy one. In 2002, we visited New Zealand. We spent nearly all of our time in Wellington but made a few short trips in the area. One of them was to the South Island. It is less developed, and its southern part is truly wild. This island has one fjord, that is, a long, narrow, winding inlet from the sea into the interior of the mainland (as in Norway). It was discovered recently and is not easily accessible. However, a tunnel was bored leading to the beginning of the fjord, where a tiny pier was built for a few small tourist boats. The inlet into this small harbor was fenced off with a net from large fish. So we took a tour on one of these boats. There were many buses, and many boats were going into the fjord one after another. We would reach the mouth of the fjord where it connected to the ocean and then sail back along the other shore. There were lots of interesting living creatures of all kinds, both on the shore and in the water, along the way. Several dolphins were swimming around. And then the following happened.

Three or four dolphins began to guide our boat. And only our boat had these maritime pilots! I don't know whether to call it luck. The people on all the other boats were looking at our boat. On them, all the people were standing on one side to see the dolphins guiding our boat. We were the only ones who had difficulty seeing them, and we were crowding the bow to look down.

So three dolphins were swimming in front of the bow of the boat the whole time (it seemed to me that there were more of them in the beginning). The boat would change its speed, but this did not affect the distance between the dolphins and the boat. Sometimes the boat would stop so that we could see other marine animals resting on the shore.

The dolphins would then swim around and wait for us. During this time, they played around the boat. And then once again they accompanied the boat in front of the bow. I was looking at a dolphin from above. One of the dolphins, who was swimming directly in front of the bow of the boat, was swimming half sideways with one eye looking at me. Maybe not only at me, but I saw its gaze. It seemed to me that the dolphin was grinning. The other two dolphins were usually swimming along the sides, at some distance. Finally, we approached the bay from which we had sailed out. Ahead of us was the net. About 50 meters before reaching the net, the dolphins rushed forward and simultaneously all three jumped out of the water, completely, high above, even at a great distance above the water, and turned in different directions. Just like they do it in a water show. But these were wild dolphins who lived in the ocean. So who could have trained them, besides their own consciousness?! All the boats were watching this. I see in this not just an attempt at contact, but a request for contact. Meanwhile, we humans are preoccupied only with our little problems.

"Thinking" Trees

Now I would like to change the "scale" of our discussion and discuss the "consciousness"/"thinking" of some huge living objects. I will talk about trees. Of course, in general, trees are so different as a species that we are unable to recognize their traces of "thinking" or "consciousness". But there are two very different kinds of trees that both show signs we can recognize. I personally had a chance to observe both of these kinds, one in the jungle of Amazon, and another in Cambodia. Perhaps there are many more, but I have only observed these two.

One of these kinds is a "walking tree". These are trees that move (walk) along the Earth surface. Not quickly — say, around five meters per year. Whoever did not know this and does not believe me, search Google for "walking tree" and see hundreds of pictures, including those that show the very process of this "walk". By the way, these are very big trees, with large trunks, that reach high into the sky. Around two meters from the ground, such a trunk is divided into lots of "branches" going down. One may think of them as roots that hang a couple of meters above the ground level. To move in a specific direction, the tree sends from its trunk above the ground new roots in the chosen direction, and when these roots firmly settle inside the soil, some roots on the opposite side, the ones no longer needed, die, and hence the whole trunk (and thus the tree) shifts in that direction. Think what kind of coordination needs to be in place in order for the trunk to remain stable and "looking up", not falling!

And where is that "brain" that regulates this? Thus, our belief that a brain is absolutely needed to "compute" and decide how to perform some clever action is wrong. This can be done without a brain. Making the choice of direction in which to move may be easier to explain. I have read that perhaps the tree needs more sun. These trees live in the tropical jungle of South America. At least this is where I saw them, and the direction in which the tree chose to move was obvious. From what I saw, it looked like the tree was trying to escape falling into a deep ravine, perhaps the result of the recent rain season

The second kind of "thinking trees" we met was in Cambodia, the so-called giant Strangling Trees.

These are huge, tremendously big trees, which live around a thousand years or more, that have completely covered, fully destroyed the old cities of Cambodia.

It was believed here that without any war, entire citadels and residencies of very powerful kings were suddenly abandoned, and the nation went to build new citadels somewhere else. These trees "eat" other trees. I have witnessed this.

The process starts with what looks like harmless lianas using the trunks of other trees for support, climbing around them and up. When such a "liana" firmly establishes itself around a neighboring trunk, it starts joining with other "lianas", turning into one formation that becomes another trunk around the trunk of this tree's "dinner tree".

After a while, it is all over for the "dinner tree", as it gets strangled and eaten. I think that at the previous stages of its growth it obtained nutrition from the tree it invaded. I have photos of all the stages of this process. But these giant trees have also destroyed buildings and huge structures in a more complicated way. However, I have difficulty explaining this in writing (see photos: on the top left photo you can see another eaten tree)

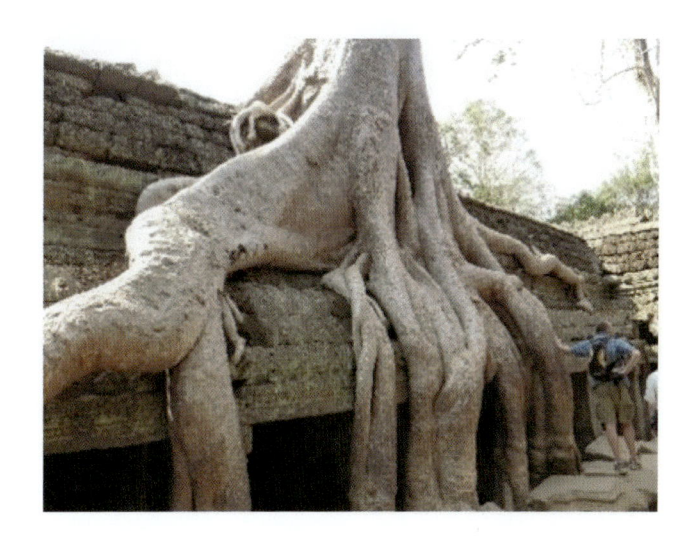

If we start to accept this point of view that forms of life other than us possess consciousness and know how to "think" and make conscious decisions, then with this view in mind, we are ready to zoom out and widen the scale of living objects.

Microflora

I'm returning to us, humans within the world of animals. It is very well known that we are not independent in our survival needs. Our stomach is full of living microorganisms, our microflora. It is very much needed for digesting food and in many other processes (say, creating certain vitamins we need).

Also, some of our own cells, like blood cells, have a semi-independent life. Our microflora does not know about our existence — it lives its own life and has its own consciousness. We may influence its existence by regulating our food, water, and possibly some other supplies. We also "defend" it from the changing conditions outside our body. It lives in very stable conditions. But it can also influence our life by developing certain illnesses or producing certain substances that may strongly influence our mood and behavior. We want to live in harmony with it, but we do not always understand how to do this (well, rather, it is very seldom that we understand this).

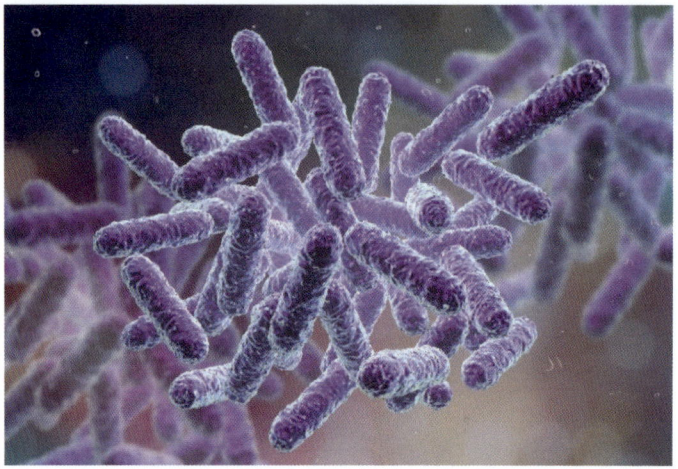

Microflora; the size of a typical microbe relates to the size of a man as the size of a man to the size of the Earth !!!

And now for some curious "measurology" (I created this word by joining "measuring" and "astrology" because, of course, the measuring I present does not prove anything, but I hope you will find it curious). Let's compare the data on microbes from our microflora with respect to us, humans, being the place of their living, with the data on us with respect to Earth, our place of living. The size of a typical individual microbe relative to the size of a typical individual person is almost exactly proportionate to our size relative to the size of the Earth! So, we live on Earth with the same space as "they" live inside us. (One may start to worry about the differences in the size of the populations; however, there are billions of different types of living forms on the surface of the Earth, as well as millions, if not more, types of microbes living inside us).

[Computation: a typical microbe is 1/10 the size of our typical cell of the body, which is around 1 micron = 10^{-6} of a meter, one over a million, i.e., for a microbe, it is 10^{-7} of one meter. Our size is around 1.7 meters. Multiplying that by 10^7, we obtain 17,000 km. But the diameter of the Earth is close to 13,000 km. The microflora of whales or elephants has even much more space inside its hosts for living than these animals have on Earth.]

And now about lifespans, the timing of our life, meaning how many generations of "our" microbes change inside us during our life. An average microbe divides every 20 to 30 minutes. Of course, for some it may take longer. And our own cells live a much longer life; say, erythrocytes live around 90 days, but then they die, not divide. So, we have around 3 (or say 2.5) generations per hour, and around 70 per day. Therefore, in one year, around 25,550 generations pass inside us, and over 80 years (it is my 80th anniversary now), we have around 2,044,000, roughly 2 million generations! To how many years of our presence on Earth could this be compared? Truly, this question doesn't make any sense from any point of view. However, I am interested in the psychological factor — the "feeling of time" of our species compared to what could be "reasonably" considered the "feeling of time" for microbes inside us.

For instance, the notion of a "generation" is different for us than for microbes, which "die" (better to say, disappear) when creating the next generation. If we simply take the span of one "generation" to equal our life expectancy (in this case, 80 years), we could say that it would take 160 million years for humans to live on Earth for as many generations as our microflora has changed inside us. However, if the "generation span" is around 25 years (the expected age of the mother at first birth), then the figure would be around 50 million years. The figures are relatively comparable. In any case, the lifespan of the microflora inside us by some objective parameters may be considered "roughly equal" to our lifespan on Earth, or at least acceptably similar.

Why do I discuss this? To state that the life on Earth may have its own consciousness. Moreover, it should have it! Of course, it should be a huge intellectual power, so great that we cannot comprehend it from our very low level of intelligence. (Can a microbe inside us understand our existence?) This approach helps to answer many wide-open questions about life. But it also creates a great number of new questions.

Cells

The next story is about the behavior of cells of a multicellular living being, the behavior that looks very conscious!

(I would like to state that all my knowledge on the life of cells I used in this chapter is from discussions with my friend, Professor of Medicine Elena (Lena) Vladimirskaya.)

Everything I recently had a chance to read on cells leads me to the following understanding:

LIFE = CONSCIOUSNESS

(i.e., there is no living object that does not have its own understanding/consciousness). This is my (conjectural) principle.

Of course, the consciousness of a specific form of life may be drastically different from what our consciousness may imagine. A lot of parameters influence it.

Let us demonstrate one case of miraculous cleverness of a cell within a multicellular living being.

One of the most incredible revelations of some 25–30 years ago was the discovery of APOPTOSIS. Again, all of my knowledge on the subject comes from our discussions with Lena. In short, apoptosis is the program inside a cell that is activated to kill it. That is, a cell may receive an order to die! This, of course, is a necessity based on the survival "instincts" of a multicellular body, e.g., such as protection from a quick cancer-related death that will most likely occur if the cells are allowed to undergo uncontrollable division. In fact, the regulation of how a cell dies should be very strict. The incredible thing is that such a program is actually continually active in a cell, always ready to act. The only way for a cell to continue living is to perform a certain function, which it is designed to keep performing. Then the action of apoptosis is delayed up until the cell starts performing something else.

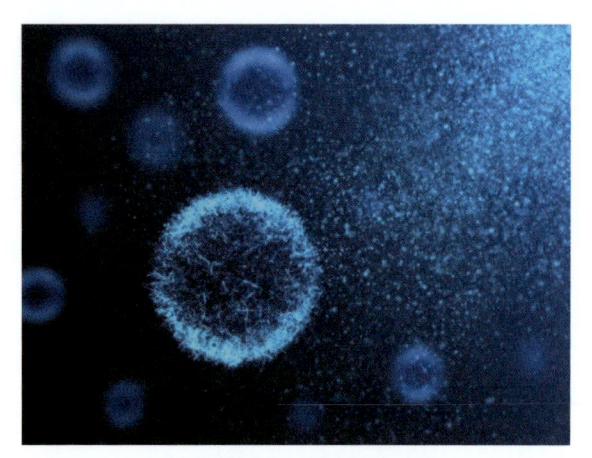

Isolated bacteria/cell

In 2020 humanity was "attacked" by the virus "Covid-19".

Below is a scientific model of this virus. The outgrowths-receptors sticking out in all directions, which look like a **crown**, gave the virus it's name "**Corona** - virus". But always remember how small it is. Its size relates to the size of a human being as a tiny ant to the size of the Earth!

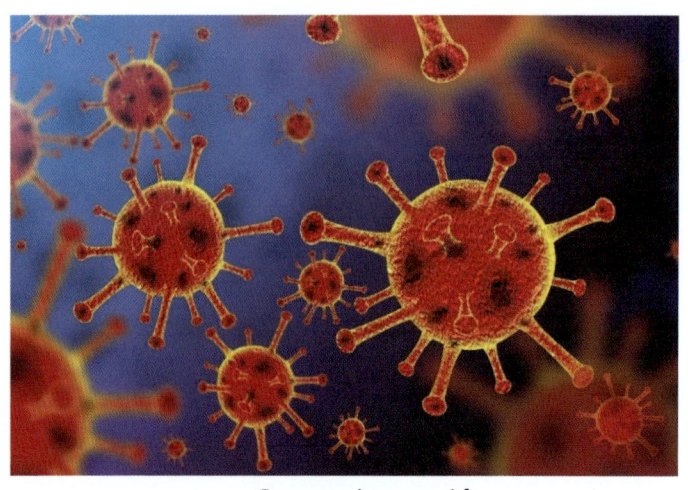

Coronavirus covid

In terms of cell size, this corona virus is like a little ant to us humans.

Let's get back to cell life.

There are two types of cell death. One is the long-known necrosis. In the event of such death, the membrane is destroyed at a very early stage in the process, and the death is always associated with external stimulation. Usually a large number of cells are involved in this process at the same time (we observe pus in this case).

The second type of death is apoptosis. In this case, the membrane is destroyed at the very end of the process, when all of its contents are, as it were, packed into the so-called apoptotic bodies that do not irritate the environment. Most often the process is genetically determined, although it can be triggered by some danger from the outside — for example, if a cell does not want to let in a virus that would multiply inside it and pose a mortal danger to other cells.

I will now illustrate how clever a cell is by demonstrating some of its actions. To be sure, I will simplify the reality. My apologies for this. On its surface, a cell has numerous receptors — their count is likely to be in the hundreds of thousands but could be below one hundred. To help us see the picture, let's imagine a cell rescaled to the size of a small town like Ramat Hasharon (where I was living recently). Then the receptors would be some structures the size of around three to five stories, on its side surface. (Let's remember that cells are three-dimensional, like a ball, and not two-dimensional, as we may perceive a city on the surface of the Earth.) Now let's imagine a molecule approaching the cell. It contains some information, which could be an order for the cell to carry out a certain action. It may enter the cell ONLY through these receptor structures (whether it is a physical intrusion or some message being delivered). The relative size of the molecule in this chosen scaling would be that of a person.

Not every receptor is ready to accept every messenger molecule — receptors are molecule-specific. And there may be no receptors at all on a given cell for some molecules. These molecules are not allowed inside and thus do not carry any information deliverable to this cell. But let's assume that there is a receptor, and a molecule has arrived that is suitable for this receptor. Now the receptor needs to make a decision as to whether or not to let it in (the molecule or the information).

Stop! Not so quickly. One single receptor will NEVER make the decision. It will either call a similar receptor located nearby, so that this receptor can move toward the original receptor, or it will create an identical receptor nearby (duplicate itself). These two receptors will then jointly make the decision.

Again, stop! Not so quickly. This scheme applies to certain "simple" decisions. If the molecule carries such a crucial order as to start apoptosis, then two receptors will not be considered good enough. Depending on the form of apoptosis, at least three receptors will be needed, and possibly as many as six of them.

Roughly speaking, there are two types of apoptosis: a slow one, which lasts many hours and can be stopped and reversed during its development, and a very quick, immediate apoptosis, which cannot be stopped after it starts. The first, the slow one, is initiated inside the cell. It is exactly like this — an order to die inside the cell, to commit suicide, due to something that went wrong inside the cell (the risk of uncontrollable division is the greatest danger for the body, in which this cell is an integral part). This is a very interesting process, which I will explain, again, in a very simplified way.

There is a certain gene in the cell that "observes" the scene. If it notices that something is wrong, it immediately stops all activity of the cell, letting it repair the system and return to normality. If this does not happen within a certain period, this gene (the "night guard", as experts call it) activates a family of genes (which I will call the "jury", as it plays this role), 16 such genes altogether, of which 10 are always pro-apoptosis (let's denote them with a "+" sign), and six are against apoptosis (I will denote them with a "-" sign). These genes produce some molecules that are involved in certain activities that end in joining these molecules into pairs. There may be pairs of (+,+), (+,-), or (-,-) type, although some may remain single. What happens next is the counting of the "votes", whereby the "lonely" (unpaired) molecules are not counted (they "did not come to vote"), and nor are the "indecisive" (+,-) pairs (abstained votes), while the (+,+) pairs count as "votes" for, and the (-,-) pairs against, apoptosis.

The majority decides the fate of the cell. (If you ask me what happens if the votes are split evenly — well, I don't know! But I suspect it is the same as a no-apoptosis vote). One may notice a more substantial problem: the *a priori* prevalence of pro-apoptosis molecules, you might think, implies a predetermined pro-apoptosis decision.

However, there is another parameter involved. These genes (the 16 genes of the "jury") produce molecules with varying ability to join another molecule from this family. Each of them has regions responsible for the ability to join another molecule. Among the six anti-apoptosis ("-" sign) molecules, four have four such regions, and the remaining two have three regions. However, among the 10 pro-apoptosis ("+" sign) molecules, only three have three regions (no molecule has four regions!), one has two such regions, and the remaining six each have only one such region!! Thus, they have a very weak ability to co-join. And this creates the balance!

If apoptosis is chosen, the other gene is activated, and a very interesting next step starts: the real "killer" gene is activated, which does the job (also very interesting). However (!!), there are some proteins that may block the action of the killer. For the whole body of cells, this is a very bad sign, since in this case the "unleashed" cell will start uncontrollable division (cancer). I will drop this part now. But what happens if the decision made is against apoptosis? Then the cell continues performing its job, the one it should be doing and was doing when it was stopped, and everything looks normal. However, our main "judge", the "night guard", may restart the process and call again for the above-described family of 16 to take another "vote" if it is still worried about something.

Quick apoptosis also may be stopped, but at a very preliminary stage of its development, the stage when the order just came in. I am not sure whether this is also programmed in the incoming order that the cell receives from the outside. So, not having any scientific justification, I will call such quick apoptosis "(a)-apoptosis", and the unconditional order to die, "(b)-apoptosis". You may have already guessed what I am going to say next. I don't know whether this is indeed so and/or already known to be true, but I think that for an (a)-apoptosis to start, it is enough to have the decision made by only three receptors. But for a quick (b)-apoptosis, six receptors are called to jointly decide!

And in any case, wouldn't you agree that cells act in a much cleverer way than we, humans, do?

I think I should feel pity for you if you still don't recognize "consciousness" in such behavior.

I will stop here. The sequel can be found in the complete book, "LIFE = CONSCIOUSNESS ; Animal consciousness, cell consciousness and other stories.

About the Author

Vitali Milman is a renowned mathematician who has published more than 200 articles and five monographs. He has received numerous prizes and is also the cofounder and co-managing editor of Geometric and Functional Analysis, one of the best mathematical journals in the world.

On the seventieth anniversary of the founding of Israel, the Milner Global Foundation selected seventy Israeli scholars who have made groundbreaking contributions in their respective fields. Vitali Milman was named as one of these most influential Israeli scientists.

Vitali is also an avid art collector.

More non-mathematics books by Vitali Milman:
- **Passion for art:** Essays on art with Russian roots
- **Three outstanding women artists:** Lydia Mandel, Ira Reichwarger, Tanya Preminger
- **Life=consciousness:** Animal consciousness, cell consciousness and other stories
- **Do Animals Think?** About consciousness in birds, dolphins, penguins, trees and other life forms (Children's book)

Printed in Great Britain
by Amazon